"God. We Need You."

A Year of Prayer in a Hospital Chapel

For the fifth Sunday after Epiphany and for days, like today, when we do not feel worthy of a calling   19

A prayer for the sixth Sunday after Epiphany and for days we face choices   21

A prayer for the seventh Sunday of Epiphany and any day we fret   23

A prayer for Transfiguration Sunday and every day when we're feeling cloudy   25

A prayer for the first Sunday in Lent   27

A prayer for the second Sunday in Lent   29

A prayer for the third Sunday in Lent   31

A prayer for the fourth Sunday in Lent and mornings when we are wondering where you are   33

A prayer for the fifth Sunday in Lent   35

A prayer for Palm Sunday that is actually a prayer for Holy Week   37

A prayer for Easter morning   39

A prayer for the second Sunday of Easter   41

A prayer for the third Sunday of Easter   43

A prayer for Mother's Day on the fourth Sunday of Easter   45

A prayer for the fifth Sunday of Easter, sort of   47

A prayer for the sixth Sunday of Easter   49

A prayer for the seventh Sunday of Easter   51

Contents

Foreword by Brian Spahr   ix

Preface   xi

A prayer for the first Sunday of Advent   1

A prayer for the second Sunday of Advent   2

A prayer for the third Sunday of Advent   4

A prayer for the fourth Sunday of Advent and Christmas   5
morning

A prayer for the last Sunday of the calendar year   7

A prayer for Epiphany   9

A prayer for the feast of the Baptism of the Lord   11

A prayer for the second Sunday after Epiphany   13

A prayer for the third Sunday after Epiphany (and days   15
when we wish we were someone else)

A prayer for the fourth Sunday after Epiphany and every   17
day that we need to reflect on love

"God. We Need You." A Year of Prayer in a Hospital Chapel

Jon Swanson

Emerald Hope Publishing House

Fort Wayne

Paperback ISBN-10: 9798646808036

Social Media Chaplain 3933 Hedwig Dr
Fort Wayne, IN 46815

Front cover photo: Portion of cross, taken by Jon Swanson, used by permission
of Patrick Riecke, Chaplaincy Director.
Author photo: Nancy Swanson

A prayer for Pentecost Sunday   53

A prayer for Trinity Sunday and the beginning of Ordinary Time   55

A prayer for the twelfth Sunday in Ordinary Time   57

A prayer for the thirteenth Sunday in Ordinary Time   59

A prayer for the fourteenth Sunday in Ordinary Time   61

A prayer for rest on the fifteenth Sunday in Ordinary Time   63

A prayer for the sixteenth Sunday in Ordinary Time   65

A prayer for seventeenth Sunday in Ordinary Time, or any time we don't understand   67

A prayer for the eighteenth Sunday in Ordinary Time   69

A prayer for the nineteenth Sunday in Ordinary Time   71

A prayer for the twentieth Sunday in Ordinary Time   73

A prayer for the twenty-first Sunday in Ordinary Time   75

A prayer for the twenty-second Sunday in Ordinary Time   77

A prayer for the twenty-third Sunday in Ordinary Time   79

A prayer for the twenty-fourth Sunday in Ordinary Time   81

A prayer for the twenty-fifth Sunday in Ordinary Time   83

A prayer on the twenty-sixth Sunday in Ordinary Time   85

A prayer for the twenty-seventh Sunday in Ordinary Time   87

A prayer for the twenty-eighth Sunday in Ordinary Time   *89*

A prayer for the twenty-ninth Sunday in Ordinary Time   *91*

A prayer for the thirtieth Sunday in Ordinary Time   *93*

A prayer for the thirty-first Sunday in Ordinary Time   *95*

A prayer for the thirty-second Sunday in Ordinary Time   *97*

A prayer for the thirty-third Sunday in Ordinary Time   *99*

A prayer for Christ the King Sunday   *101*

Afterword by Fr. James Bromwich   *103*

About the Author   *106*

Resources on Faith, Sickness, Grief, and Doubt   *108*

Foreword by Brian Spahr

Earlier this week I lost a dear friend. He was diagnosed with cancer a few weeks ago. Early Saturday morning I awoke to a phone call from his daughter with the news that he had died. As a hospital chaplain, I'm around death often. I know how to be present for others in their grief and loss, but this week I've been struggling with my own. It had also been a tough week at the hospital which only compounded my grief. I struggled to pray. What words could express how my heart was crying out? No words came. Then my friend Jon handed me a short prayer he had written for a project at the hospital. His words put language to what I couldn't say on my own at that moment or since.

Prayer is powerful. Jon's prayer has certainly helped me in my grief. I've seen and experienced God's power and presence and peace countless times through prayer. But prayer often remains hard for me. It's not only when I'm struggling. I'm a pastor and a hospital chaplain, so I pray all the time with, and for, people. I know what to say and what not to say. And yet, most people never notice when they listen to me that I don't always have confidence in doing so. I often struggle to find language that matches the prayers of my heart. I get too stuck in my head. It feels like by the time the words reach my lips, they no longer express the real and raw prayers inside me. This is one of the reasons I am so thankful for Jon and for this book.

I started meeting with Jon as my spiritual director a few years ago. He has a knack for helping me listen well to the Spirit, and he challenges me to respond. In our conversations, Jon would often reference his daily writing at 300wordsaday.com. I don't read many blogs, but I read Jon, especially on Sundays. Each Sunday, Jon posts a prayer to go along with the lectionary reading for the day. Many of those prayers became the prayers found in this book. In many of these prayers, I've found the language I'm so often searching for. I've leaned on these words in my private prayer life. I've shared them publicly in worship gatherings and on social media. I'm thrilled now to have them together in this collection. I know in these words you will find language for the prayers of your heart as well.

Thank you, Jon, for your friendship. Thank you for your partnership in ministry. Thank you for taking the time to listen to the Spirit and to help me do the same. Thank you for these prayers.

+++

Brian Spahr is pastor of Come2Go Ministries (Fort Wayne), a chaplain at Parkview Health System, and a husband and dad.

Preface

Some hospitals convert closets to chapels by adding a table and a Bible and a chair. Our hospital chapel is deceptively beautiful. We have simple stained glass, wood walls, upholstered chairs, designed colors. There are fifty chairs and a keyboard. There is a blown-glass font, a small side chapel where the Tabernacle holds the host for the Catholic masses.

It is a beautiful, quiet, calming space, where I once found a woman weeping at the base of the stained glass cross. We prayed. Her child eventually recovered. But it's a constant reminder that in hospitals, beauty and pain are always present.

Each Sunday, I stand in that chapel. Nancy, my wife, plays a brief prelude. I welcome the people watching the service live or by recording. I read a psalm, we sing one or two verses of an old hymn. I read the reading from the Old Testament, and a reading from the New Testament. And then I pray.

When I started as a hospital chaplain, I didn't write out my prayers. I'm from a tradition that is more spontaneous. But somewhere along the line, I realized that I wasn't very coherent in my spontaneous prayers. Because I'm a hospital chaplain. And on any given Sunday morning, before the service I've talked to a family expecting their loved one to die before the day is over. I've responded to the Emergency Department where a person heading to church ran off the road. I've been part of a search for family for someone who has no one close. I know that before the day is over, my colleagues and I will witness death.

So I started writing my prayers.

+++

I have a confession.

I wanted to be theological and scholarly in this preface. I wanted to talk about public pastoral prayer in a way that is thoughtful and profound.

I wanted to explore the Biblical history of people who stand in front of groups of God's people and lead them in prayer. Nehemiah, who taught me about private and public prayer.[1] Mary, who composed the Magnificat during a long walk to her relative's house. The Apostles, crying out to God for boldness after being threatened by the rulers, elders, and teachers of the law. Jesus, who gave the disciples training wheels for prayer and provided unknown examples and a handful of recorded models.

I wanted to talk about the way that prayer changes when it is public. Public prayer often feels like a mixture of performance and preaching for-or at-an audience. And, in truth, it is a little of both.

1. I wrote about my conversations with Nehemiah in *A Great Work*.

The presence of an audience always changes communication. And I wanted to go to my roots as a rhetorical scholar to explore what is happening.[2]

I wanted to reflect on what might be happening when in prayer we "have come to Mount Zion, to the city of the living God, the heavenly Jerusalem. You have come to thousands upon thousands of angels in joyful assembly, to the church of the firstborn, whose names are written in heaven. You have come to God, the Judge of all, to the spirits of the righteous made perfect, to Jesus the mediator of a new covenant, and to the sprinkled blood that speaks a better word than the blood of Abel."[3]

I confess. I wanted to measure up to the great thinkers and writers and practitioners on prayer. I wanted to get this right.

But at its best, public, pastoral prayer, isn't a scholarly pursuit. It stands in a humble, holy place in the presence of God and the people. The person leading the prayers of the people is giving voice to the deepest needs and desires of a group of people who felt those things but couldn't name them. The person leading the prayers is giving them permission to feel those needs and desires. The person leading the prayers is revealing some of the brokenness of being human.

And so, this book isn't a scholarly work. It's a collection of the prayers lived and offered during a year of Sundays in a hospital chapel by a hospital chaplain.

2. My PhD is in rhetorical theory and criticism, not theology. So I think often about prayer and the Bible from a communication with God perspective.
3. Hebrews 12:22-24.

In our chapel services, we use the Revised Common Lectionary to determine the Biblical texts for each week.[4] And we follow the liturgical year, starting with the first Sunday of Advent. The structure connects our services to the services people may be missing in their home church, if they have one. And for those who have no congregation and are in the hospital for an average of four days, it still gives a structure.

Every Saturday, I look at the texts and I think about the death and illness and injury that have been present in the rooms of our hospital, in the lives of the people I've talked with and prayed with. In my own life.

Every Saturday, I take a pen or a keyboard, and I start to talk with God about what I and others feel, what I and others confess, what I and others ought to know about God but don't actually believe.

As I talk with God on Saturday, I am aware that I don't know what will be happening when I read these words at 10:30 on Sunday morning in a hospital chapel. Death, stillbirth, heart attack have all happened early on Sunday mornings. And so, I do my best to be honest. To remember promises instead of platitudes. To be trusting. To acknowledge doubt. To ask for peace that is miraculous because it doesn't make any sense in these moments. To lament and confess and draw close.

---

4. A lectionary is a schedule of Bible readings most often arranged according the liturgical calendar. For each Sunday, there is a Psalm, and readings from the Old Testament, the Epistles, and the Gospels. The readings are in a three year cycle. The authoritative print source is *The Revised Common Lectionary: Twentieth Anniversary Annotated Edition* (Minneapolis: Fortress Press), 2012. A web version of the lectionary is at https://lectionary.library.vanderbilt.edu/

Every Saturday, after I talk with God as I write, I put the prayer in my notes for Sunday, and I put it in a blog post at 300wordsaday.com, to be shared early Sunday morning with a group of faithful readers. Because public pastoral prayer needs to be heard and joined by people. And there are online friends who will keep me honest.

This book is a collection of the written prayers offered on behalf of myself and the people in the rooms during one year, Year C in the Lectionary.

Some notes and acknowledgements:

I was not in the chapel on three Sundays during this year, but I included the prayers I offered online for those weeks.

I am grateful to Nancy for coming to chapel every week and for walking through life together since 1982, even during those times this year when she couldn't walk. Nancy and I live through and process the experiences and faith reflected in these prayers.

I am grateful to Patrick Riecke, Teresa Wedler, and Lydia Miller who hired me as a chaplain and then assigned me to Sundays. And have built a remarkable chaplaincy team. And for Patrick including me in the "Resources on Faith, Sickness, Grief and Doubt." Patrick, Kristen, and I are building a helpful set of tools together.

I am grateful to Parkview Health System for remarkable coworkers and resources. The intercessions and opinions in these prayers are my own work and do not necessarily reflect Parkview.

I'm grateful to Brian Spahr and Father James Bromwich for being friends and being willing to write the Foreword and Afterword. Father James taught me that when Catholics didn't raise their heads when I finished p raying i n t heir r ooms, I n eeded t o say "Through Christ our Lord." And I'm grateful for Jen Bradbury's blurb. Jen's passion for considering our Christology guides me more than she knows. Until now.

I'm grateful to Hope Swanson Smith for that last format alignment of titles and punctuation. And for coffee and walks and a (your) lifetime of being dad and daughter.

I am grateful to God for listening.

A prayer for the first Sunday of Advent

God, we light candles when it is light,
knowing that when it is dark,
the light that is little now
will be large then.

We speak your words of promise when it is light,
knowing that when it is dark,
the promises that are easy to say now,
will be anchors to hold onto.
Amen.

A prayer for the second Sunday of Advent

God.

I am supposed to have answers and clarity and direction. I am supposed to offer structure and encouragement and order. I am supposed to. And I cannot. Or better, at the moment, in this moment, I have few words, little clarity.

I have, we all have been through weeks that are overwhelming. We have worked long hours. We have faced separation, death, diagnosis, depression, and hundreds of little things that simply didn't work.

We confess that we turn to comparing struggles, looking at how my week was worse that your week, how my dread is worse than your dread.

We confess that we try to be gracious, ignoring our own struggles because others seem worse, and thereby doing more damage to ourselves.

We acknowledge that as we turn toward comparison, we isolate ourselves from each other and from you. We confess that we are wrapped with layers of past pain and current mistrust and anticipation of a future of more of the same.

What we want to be true is that you, who gives us endurance and encouragement, would draw us together.

God of hope, fill us with joy and peace. Help us trust in you. Help us not depend on our own attempts at motivation or inspirational posters or wise sayings.

Instead, let us overflow with hope by the power of your Holy Spirit.

Because of what was written in the past about you and your work and your promises, help us to turn our minds and tune our hearts to you. Help us know the words of the law and the prophets and the apostles.

Or better, help us listen to David and Isaiah and Paul and Matthew, people who lived lives, who got angry, who felt fear, who saw death, and who learned to trust in you. In their stories, in your words, we will find encouragement and endurance and hope.

We ask through Christ our Lord.

Amen.

A prayer for the third Sunday of Advent

God of heaven and earth,
we know that we want joy
and are called to rejoice
and are offered examples of rejoicing.

God of heaven and earth,
we know that we have fatigue
and wander into uncertainty
and see examples of pain and struggle.

Today we light a candle called joy.
We ask you to use its light
to help us see you as a guiding glimmer,
to offer joy to our fatigue
and rejoicing to our uncertainty,
and to sustain us in our struggle.

Amen.

A prayer for the fourth Sunday of Advent and Christmas morning

God of forever and God of this moment,

you watch and work
from ancient times,
in now, and
for ever.

We only live now.

We light candles.
We say "I love you".
We lie down and get up.

Tiny actions in this moment that feel almost useless sometimes.

They would be if not for you
who gave us light,
who gives us love,
who laid down your life and got up.

At Advent we do our best to remember that you were and are and will be.

And we pray that you forgive us when we forget.

And this candle we light to remember.

Amen

A prayer for the last Sunday of the calendar year

God.

We sit at the transition from one year to the next.

Part of us hopes that things will be different.
Part of us knows that things never are.
Part of us hopes that we will be different.
Part of us fears that we never will be.
Part of us knows that you are all-powerful,
all-knowing, all-present.
Part of us isn't at all sure that applies to our lives,
our problems, our cares.
Part of us wants to know the peace you promise,
a peace that we can't even understand.
Part of us is anxious that it won't be there, and then we will be
stuck.

Jesus, you've heard this before.

You heard a man say "I do believe; help me overcome my

unbelief!"
You heard followers say, "You are the Christ. Where else would we go?" and then they went.

You have heard it all. And you stick around.

God Almighty, Lord of heaven and earth,
Spirit of the Living God,
Creator, Redeemer, Sustainer

Help me, help us, in this transition from one year to the next, to bring our parts together in your power and presence.
Bring healing to our hearts, to our bodies, to our relationships with each other and you.
Restore unto us the joy of our salvation.
Renew us by the power of your Spirit.

Amen.

A prayer for Epiphany

God.

You know more of the story than I do. More of my story. More of our stories.

You know what has happened and what is happening and what will happen.

We read about wise men meeting you, Jesus, after a long journey. They saw you, they honored you, they went on their journey back home.

They didn't know the whole story, but they trusted what they knew.

The time-span on their story is beyond our imagination.

Isaiah heard you and repeated your words.

Micah heard you and repeated your words.

Those words made sense in talking about you, Jesus.

I don't have centuries, God. The needs that we face for the lives of loved ones and ourselves are measured in moments, not centuries. If we have to wait, we'll all be gone.

But your big story, of the long-predicted, long-anticipated, lived-in-real-time birth and life and death and resurrection and ascension and return of Jesus gives hope and meaning for our short stories.

We talk with you today, and because of that long story, you sometimes answer today.

And you always want to visit with us, to hear our requests, to comfort our affliction, to help us find meaning in our hardest moments.

Work with us today, I ask.
Give us your wisdom, your peace.
And your reminders that in centuries or in minutes, you are aware and working.

In the name of Jesus we ask you for these things.

Amen.

+++

Isaiah 60:1-6; Ephesians 3:1-21

A prayer for the feast of the Baptism of the Lord

God.

We need a blessing,
spoken right to us, using our name.

"My son, my daughter, I've called you by name. You are mine."

Because we need to belong to someone. Irrevocably. Irretrievably.

We think we want, we've been told we want,
the blessing of stuff.

We tell each other that your blessing is health,
that it is bills paid, that it is the relief of problems.

But we confess that, when we think carefully,
sometimes we are blessed in the absence of stuff and
are cursed in the absence of challenge.

We confess that we value the release we want you to give us
more than the Spirit that you want to give us.

But we want your Spirit, the seal of your presence, the blessing of you naming us.

We want to be drenched in the waters of baptism, symbolically washed clean.

Remind us today of your power and love and presence, three-person God.

Amen.

+++

Isaiah 43:1–7; Acts 8:14–17; Luke 3

A prayer for the second Sunday after Epiphany

God.

We read about miracles in the Bible. People healed. People fed. Water turned into wine.

We want those kinds of miracles. Because people are sick. People are hungry. We'd just love to have a great celebration.

We don't see those miracles.

Maybe we could help people out. Offer them courage. Offer them opportunities. Maybe we could offer shoveling and comfort and supper.

But those aren't *you* doing a miracle; those are *us* expressing love.

Which is, I suppose, a kind of miracle. Or at least a kind of obedience, offering love to people who need it, in the ways that we best do it. As cooks and caregivers, as hard workers, and as calm speakers, as open-hearted listeners, and open-mouthed defenders.

We confess that we ignore opportunities,
because we are waiting for you to take the first step.
We confess that we take the gifts you give,
and we don't share them with those who could use them.
We confess that we don't confess our weakness and accept your strength.

Thank you for your forgiveness.
Thank you for your work through the people we will see today.
Help us see you in them.
And bless them as they bless us.

Amen.

+++

Isaiah 62:1-5; 1 Corinthians 2:1-11; John 2:1-11

A prayer for the third Sunday after Epiphany (and days when we wish we were someone else)

God.

We know that we are not like each other.

We look different,
we do different things,
we feel different feelings.

We confess that often,
we wish you had made us like someone else.
We confess that often,
we wish you had made other people like us.
And we acknowledge that we just wish that people liked us.
And that we liked them.

It's harder, the gap between who we are and who others are
when we are in moments of pain and uncertainty.
Fear and sickness make our thinking and feeling hard.

We are not who we want to be.
We react how we wish we didn't.
We confess.

God, here's what we ask.
We ask you to help us understand the differences that you created,
the differences that you built into us
to be helpful for each other,
to be challenging to each other,
to learn to be loving of each other.

Help us suffer with those who suffer.
Help us honor those who are being honored.
Help us be a body that cares for itself rather than a body that destroys itself.
Help us proclaim your truth rather than our divisions.
Help us love as you have loved.

Help us know your love.

We ask this of you, God, because Jesus invited us to.

Amen.

+++

Nehemiah 8:1-10; 1 Corinthians 12:12-31; Luke 4

A prayer for the fourth Sunday after Epiphany and every day that we need to reflect on love

God.

You invite us into relationship with you.
You send us to do your work.

We don't feel worthy of either one. Except sometimes.

Sometimes we expect you to help us do your work on *our* terms.
We demand your love on *our* terms.
We say, "If you really loved us, you would fix this, you would change them, you would leave me alone."
We say, "I'm doing this for you, so you should do that for me."

We say that we can't believe in a God like we are told you are.

But when we stop and talk with you, we have much to confess.

We confess that we are not the ones who get to decide what your love is; you are.

We confess that we are not the ones who get to decide what your work is; you are.
We confess that we like telling you what you should do
more than we like receiving your words of challenge and comfort and compassion.
And we confess that we don't really believe that you have already forgiven us.

God, you are patient and kind.
You don't envy or boast.
You bear all things,
believe all things,
hope all things,
endure all things.

We know that because you, Jesus, did that.
All the way to the cross and beyond.

God, help us to love with your love, to work with your strength, to speak your words, to wait in your silence.

God, help us.

Amen.

+++

Jeremiah 1; 1 Corinthians 13; Luke 4

For the fifth Sunday after Epiphany and for days, like today, when we do not feel worthy of a calling

God.

Isaiah wrote your words in a scroll. He wrote more words than almost anyone else in the Old Testament. And the words he wrote down are quoted throughout the New Testament.

Paul wrote your words in letters that we still read, over and over. His letters shape much of our thinking about what church could be.

Peter wrote some more of the New Testament. And he was also the leader in the earliest days of the church.

And all three of them talk about how insignificant and unworthy they are.

If they aren't any good, how can we hope to be useful to you or to anyone? How can we hope to measure up, hope to be any good?

19

If they aren't worthy of being called by you, famous leaders and authors that they were, what hope is there for us?

Unless.

Unless it's really true that you start with what we are and you fill us with your words, and you forgive us with your graciousness, and you welcome us with your deep love.

But how can that be true?

We confess that we question your judgment.
We confess that we live more comfortably in our sense of insignificance than in your welcoming power.
We confess that we are afraid you might expect more from us than we can imagine doing.

Forgive us.

And remind us that in our weakness, you are strong.
Remind us that in our lack of words, you are the loving Word.
Remind us that you overlook our gaps, and you fill us with your fullness.
Remind us that you want us.

We ask through Christ our Lord.
May it be so.

+++

Isaiah 6:1-13; 1 Corinthians 15:1-11; Luke 5:1-11

A prayer for the sixth Sunday after Epiphany and for days we face choices

God.

We aren't very good with choices. It's hard to choose between the best thing for us and the best thing for others.

Choosing the right voices to listen to is hard. There are so many voices and so many options and so many things going wrong.

Choosing the right people to follow is hard. There are so many people who claim to be right and so many people who mess up. Including ourselves.

And then we struggle with deciding between trusting you and trusting ourselves.

We confess that we are not enough.
We confess that our choices are disappointing to us, to those we love.
We confess that we think that our choices are disappointing to you.

We confess that we don't understand how you look at us very well at all.

Forgive our disbelief.
Search our hearts and help us know your love.
Give us peace to listen *to* you.
Give us discernment to know that it *is* you.
Give us courage to follow you.

Help us stand strong.
Hold us when we are weak.
Hear our prayer, we ask.
And let us know you do hear.

Amen.

+++

Jeremiah 17:5-10; 1 Corinthians 15:12-20; Luke 6:17-26

A prayer for the seventh Sunday of Epiphany and any day we fret

God.

We tell ourselves and each other to be still before you. We tell each other and ourselves to be patient.

We hear that those who do evil will not last, but we can't be still and be patient when there is so much anger and fear, when there are people losing their lives because of our inhumanity. Or maybe because of our humanity.

We beg you for justice and deliverance, begging like Joseph must have begged, year after year after year, betrayed by brothers, alone in Egypt.

And yet, when he saw his brothers, he welcomed them and kissed them. He gave them hope and a future.

We confess that we are unwilling to forgive such deep pain so quickly.
We confess that we are sometimes unwilling to forgive

inconveniences just on principle.

We confess that our anger and worry are often evidence that we do not trust you. We do not trust you with our reputation, with our well-being, with our families, with our future.

Today, forgive us our trespasses
as we forgive those who trespass against us.
Forgive what we owe you
as we forgive what we believe others owe us.
Let us know our salvation and deliverance are from you.

And let us know your salvation and deliverance from our fears and fretting *now*.

May it be so.

+++

Psalm 137; Genesis 45:3-11; Luke 6:27-38

A prayer for Transfiguration Sunday and every day when we're feeling cloudy

God.

Most of us don't glow.

We talk to you, sometimes, with grief and questions, with confidence and confusion, with hopes and fears for ourselves and others. When we say "amen" and turn to the people near us, we don't need to put a mask over our faces to keep them from being blinded. We seldom look in the mirror and think, "I've got a special glow." So when we read about Moses needing to cover his face, we're not sure what to think.

We want to believe it's possible that as we talk with you, the very conversation changes us. We want to believe that we can become more and more like you. We confess that we aren't sure how that happens.

We confess that we're not sure we spend enough time with you to have it happen.

We confess that sometimes we even focus more on our confession than we do on the relationship your forgiveness invites.

You love us. You really love us.
You want to talk with us about what's been and what is and what will be.
You want to talk with us about who we've been and who we are and who we will be.

You want to talk with us.
With us. Not *at* us.
Not us at you. With us.

Would you help us, by the power of your Spirit, to think about your glory?
About the glory of your self-sacrificial love?
About the glory of your holy motives and pure plans?
About the glory of your us-welcoming, us-washing, us-transforming, us-lifting love?
And, if it please you, *could we have a little of that glory linger on our faces as we turn back to our daily lives?*

May it be so.

Amen.

+++

Exodus 34:29-35; 2 Corinthians 13:12-4:2

A prayer for the first Sunday in Lent

God.

Sometimes we simply don't know what you want.

If we knew, for sure, we'd do it. Maybe.

But we feel like we don't know what you want. And we worry that we will do the wrong thing, or the right thing for the wrong reasons. We worry about keeping you happy and not making you mad. We worry.

If we don't keep you happy, you won't do the things that make us happy. Like healing our loved one. Like giving us work. Like fixing our relationships.

So we try to make you happy and then we get mad when you don't fix things.

We confess.
We confess that we haven't spent time listening to you so we know what you want.
We confess that we haven't spent time turning away from other

voices so we can hear yours.

We confess that we haven't spent time learning how you lived, Jesus, so we can live like you.

We confess that we don't confess that God raised you from the dead.

We confess that we forget that you are involved at all.

But because you are God and are raised from the dead, you forgive us for what we confess.

You invite us to follow you in our weakness and forgetfulness.

You offer to be our God because we fail at being god.

I ask on our behalf that you will help us remember the story of you and your love and your forgiveness.

Help us say no and say yes.

And Jesus, give us strength after losing one hour of sleep the way you had strength after 40 days without food in the desert.

Amen.

+++

Deuteronomy 26:1-11; Romans 10:8-13; Luke 4:1-13

A prayer for the second Sunday in Lent

God.

You and we make promises.

Maybe that's part of what it means to be a person, to make promises to other people. Commitments. Covenants. Agreements. We agree to belong to each other. We agree to belong to teams, to communities, to congregations. We say that we will keep faith.

And then we don't.

We confess that we willfully choose to do things that we know are not for the good of those we are committed to.
We confess that we unwittingly make choices that damage our relationships.
We confess that we often do not live as if we await a savior.
We confess that we often believe that you will break your promises to us as easily as we break our promises to you.

But you won't.

Jesus, your promise to never leave us or forsake us doesn't depend on us or our behavior. Your promises to give us peace as we pray, to give us wisdom as we ask, to teach us your ways, to forgive our sins, your promises do not end.

And so today, we confess our sins, and we accept your forgiveness.
We confess our doubts, and we accept your certainty.
We confess our turmoil, and we accept your peace.
We confess our uncertainty, and we request your wisdom.

Thank you for your gentle probing that reveals our failures.
Thank you that the screaming condemnation is not you.

May we today know your peace.

Amen.

+++

Genesis 15:1–12, 17–18; Philippians 3:17–4:1; Luke 13:31–35

A prayer for the third Sunday in Lent

God.

We think of you often as angry,
and we want to think of you as loving.
We think of you as loving,
and we want to think of you as non-judgmental.
We think of you as non-judgmental,
and we want to think of you as, well, as shallowly nice.

We read texts that talk about your boundless graciousness and
others that talk about people falling into the ground and being
killed by snakes. And we aren't sure what to think about you.

We confess that we want you to be like us more than we want
you to be like you.
We confess that we are uncertain where your boundaries are so
that we have created our own and blamed them on you.
We confess that we have assumed that some definitions of evil
were made by people. Therefore we've assumed that *all* definitions
of evil are made by people, not you.

And we confess that we have given up on you for reasons that are comfortable for us.

We have all sinned, and we all fall short of your glory.

But you offer justice, as in appropriate judgment. And you don't stop just with judgment.
You offer forgiveness, you offer healing, you offer relief from temptation, you offer mercy.
You offer relationship with you, with the one who understands, who creates, who heals, who redeems, who makes all things new.

Teach us your ways.
Strengthen us to follow them.
Teach us to offer compassion and mercy, and leave judgment to you.
Because you can balance justice and mercy perfectly. And we can't.
And shouldn't, perhaps, even try.
Until we have your mind and heart and thoughts and love flowing through us.

Thank you for you.

Amen.

+++

Isaiah 55:1-9; 1 Corinthians 10:1-13; Luke 13:1-9

A prayer for the fourth Sunday in Lent and mornings when we are wondering where you are

God.

We are here.
You are there.

We are not sure where *here* is, if we are honest. We watch the seasons change, we watch our parents change, our children change. We lose jobs and friends, we change houses and towns, we find callings and cancer. And we feel lost.

And we are not sure where *there* is. We point up when we talk about heaven, pointing to the man upstairs, pointing to the sky. But we know that Jesus said he would be with us always.

So we are here.
You are here.
But we're not sure where you are.

We confess.

We confess that we lose track of who you have said we are.

We confess that we lose track of why you love us, or even *that* you love us.

We confess that we drift from you, we run from you, we define you to fit our desires, we make you in our image.

We confess that we struggle to be your ambassador, because we can't remember who or what we are really supposed to represent.

We confess that we do things that aren't right, and we don't do things that are right.

We confess.

But we also confess that Jesus is Lord.

And though we are inarticulate ambassadors, you are drawing us back to you, giving us courage in the middle of fear, giving us peace in the middle of uncertainty, giving us home when we wander away.

You love us more than we love you. Which is a really good thing. You trust us with your story even when you know we speak it poorly,

Which may be the story after all.

That your love isn't about how good we are but about how good you are.

Give us your peace, again, for today.

Amen.

+++

Joshua 5:9-12; 2 Corinthians 5:16-21; Luke 15:1-3, 11-32

A prayer for the fifth Sunday in Lent

God.

Can we call you that? Can we start that way?

Do we have to say, "Dear God" in order for you to hear us?

Or is it "Dear Jesus" or "Dear God Almighty, maker of heaven and earth"?

Do we have to tell you everything we have done wrong before we can ask you for something good?

Do we have to get the words right to get you to do something?

We confess that we're not sure.

We confess that we want you to do a new thing,

but that scares us.

We confess that we might not want to have to change, that we might not trust you enough to let go of everything we've put together. Even though we know that we aren't very put together. We confess, right now, that we are pretty scared. Scared of holding on, of letting go, of pushing hard, of pushing too hard. Scared of you.

We confess that we are not like Paul. We don't want to know you with every ounce of our being.

We confess.

But we know that you want us to know you.

We know that you want to forgive us, that, in fact, you have already forgiven us even before we ask. That, in fact, you, Jesus, came and died and rose to offer that forgiveness, to show how much you want us to know you.

Help us, please, to live as if we are forgiven.
Help us, please, to live as if the God of the Universe wants to talk to us.
Help us, please, to live in whatever that new thing is that you are wanting to do.

Because we're not doing great in the old thing we are trying to do.

Thanks.

+++

Isaiah 43:16-21; Philippians 3:4-14

A prayer for Palm Sunday that is actually a prayer for Holy Week

God.

We call this Holy Week. We try to figure out new things to say, or new things to feel about all that happened during this week. Jesus was celebrated. Jesus turned over money tables. Jesus debated and won. Jesus washed feet. Jesus started what we call communion. Jesus gave the disciples a summary of the heart of his teaching. Jesus taught us about you, Spirit.

And then Jesus was betrayed, was mocked, was crucified, was stabbed, was buried.

In this week Jesus gave up being in charge. He gave himself up to you, God, and was acted upon by everyone around him.

When we feel acted upon by everyone around us, we react. We defend. We demand. We despair. We deny. In other words, we are exactly unlike your mindset, Jesus.

We confess.

We confess that we want to be right, even when you are.
We confess that we want to be in control, even when you are.
We confess that we want to be adequate, even when you are.
We confess that we are not humble, we are not willing, we are not quiet, we are not open.

And yet.

And yet, knowing who we are and how we are, you understood why we are that way. And you became obedient to death on our behalf.

This week, God, please make this week holy.

Fill it fresh with you.

Help us listen.

We ask this because of your forgiveness and your relationship.

Amen.

+++

Luke 19:28–40; Philippians 2:5–11

A prayer for Easter morning

God.

It is Easter.
It is Resurrection Day.
It is a massive celebration of new life and bunnies,
Peeps and people singing,
chocolate and resurrection,
new dresses and empty grave clothes.
It is a day of arguing over how to celebrate you and how to find
you and who has the best party.

It is, we confess, a really confusing day.

We confess that we want to celebrate you,
but we often celebrate us.
We confess that we want to understand resurrection,
but we want to resurrect ourselves.
We confess that we know you make all things new,
but we're not sure we can afford to give up the old. The
familiarity, the comfort, the identity.

We confess that we know you offer forgiveness,
but we're not sure we want to admit we need it.

Thank you for your patience with us.
Thank you that while we were not worth dying for, in our eyes,
you died for us and rose again.
Because you want us to be your friends, your children, your body.

Help us today to know our failings,
then your forgiveness,
then your love for us,
then fellowship with you and each other.

Help us not get stuck in our crud, in our sense of obligation.
Help us today to acknowledge that with you we have life.
Even when we are here in a hospital, wrestling with the realization
of death.

Help us, we ask.

Amen.

+++

Acts 10:34-43; 1 Corinthians 15:19-26

A prayer for the second Sunday of Easter

God.

In the busyness of this week I forgot that last weekend we talked about the resurrection of Jesus, about the invitation to relationship you offer.

Some of us committed ourselves to being more aware of the forgiveness you offer and the peace that you provide and the possibility of living without so much fear. That's what we thought in the excitement of Sunday.

And then the work of Monday showed up. And we forgot.

We confess that we ignore you when you tell us "be not afraid."
We confess that we ignore you when you tell us that you are with us always.
We confess that we find it hard to believe that you love us and have freed us and have made us a kingdom.
We confess that we are more interested in building our own kingdoms than learning to live in yours.
We confess that our attention is consumed by the kingdoms of

this world, with all their arguments and attacks and opinions and distractions.

We confess.

But again and again you remind us that once and for always you forgave and freed us.

And at this moment, you tell us, that if we forgive sins, they are forgiven, in your name and in your power and for your glory.

Help us remember your forgiveness.
Help us delight in your love.
Help us work for the good of your kingdom.

Even today in this place.
Wherever this place may be, and whenever today is.

Amen.

+++

John 20:19-31; Acts 5:27-32; Revelation 1:4-8

A prayer for the third Sunday of Easter

God.

We are a little afraid of you. Some people I know are angry about you.

You don't answer their prayer. And you answer the prayer of other people. And people who don't even pray get what they want. That doesn't seem right.

And you act really angry sometimes. At least we read that in the Bible. And so, people say that if you are the kind of God that swallows up people in the ground, they don't want to believe in you.

Sometimes I understand what they are saying, even if I don't agree with them. Because it takes explaining to understand the ground opening up.

We confess that we don't understand.
We confess that we don't like you sometimes.
We confess that we don't understand you ever.
We confess that we think we understand you often.

JON SWANSON

We confess that we are caught between doubt and fear and hopefulness and uncertainty.

But also, we are challenged, Jesus, by your graciousness to the ones who killed you and to people like Paul who wanted to kill your followers.

We would love to know that you aren't angry with us, that you hear us, that you are with us.

We would love to be sure that when you say, "follow me", it's an invitation to be with you, not a scolding obligation.

We would love to rest in the knowledge that you know best and love best and care most and protect us.

Because we would love to rest in you.

Help us.

Forgive us.

Comfort us.

Strengthen us.

Let us rest in you, Immanuel, God with us.

Amen.

+++

Acts 9:1-20; Revelation 5:11-14; John 21:1-19

A prayer for Mother's Day on the fourth Sunday of Easter

God.

We are in a hospital on Mother's Day. We need to have tears wiped away from our eyes. None of us wants to be here. Except, perhaps, for those in the Family Birthing Center who have just been through labor and are holding a newborn, healthy and squalling or content.

For them we rejoice and are grateful.

The rest of us are working rather than celebrating, worrying about treatments, anticipating what may happen before the end of the day.

We're missing mothers who are gone or who have never been around.

We grieve the loss of children and of opportunities.

We usually confess something here, God, some ways that we

have fallen short. But on Mother's Day, most of us have a deep awareness of those ways.

And so I ask for healing.

I ask that you will make my sisters aware of your sufficiency and theirs.
I ask that you will make my sisters aware of your grace and theirs.
I ask that you will make us all aware of your forgiveness for what we have done and haven't done.
I ask that you will make us aware of who we are, so we do not constantly lament who we are not.
I ask that you will make us all aware of ways that we can offer your love and ours, your healing and ours, your presence and ours, to those who need it.

May it be so.

+++

Acts 9:36-43; Revelation 7:9-17; John 10:22-30

A prayer for the fifth Sunday of Easter, sort of

God.

Every Sunday morning, I talk to you in front of a group, on behalf of a group. I respond to the texts for the day. I acknowledge—so that *we* can acknowledge—our best wishes, our worst behaviors. Not specific acts out loud but specific patterns. Our lack of trust, our inconsistent faithfulness.

But I'm not in chapel this Sunday morning.

At the very time I would be reading and praying and leading, I'm in a plane. With a bird's eye view of the coast and the clouds and the crazy quilt pattern of people.

I almost called it a God's eye view. But this altitude and terrain isn't what you see.

You see people. Always, you see people. Worried, chattering, sleeping, self-distracting, expectant, hesitant people.

So where I see creation from 30,000 feet, you see my response to your work, appreciation or deprecation, consumption or stewardship, delight in the interplay of hilltops and water vapor or mere distraction from my real work. You look at my heart and the hearts of the rest of us in this plane.

This week, God, I'll be at a conference with rooms full of chaplains. My family and friends will be about their work, or looking for work, or retired from work. We will be rejoicing and lamenting, working (too much) and resting (not enough). We will be tempted to think of you look at us from 30,000 feet or from a million miles away.

But you are Immanuel, God with us. You are the one who promises that you will never leave us or forsake us. You are the Spirit who fills us, who broods over creation like a mother hen rather than a critic.

Would you bless us this week, with faith rather than fear?

May it be so.

A prayer for the sixth Sunday of Easter

God.

We do not like to wait.

We do not like to wait in line. To wait for answers. To wait for medicine to work, to wait for the end to come, to wait for the beginning to start.

Which means that we do not like to be where we are most of the time.

We do not like to be out of control, to be at the mercy of others.

We confess.

We confess that we don't like to be at your mercy.
We confess that we aren't sure about your control.
We confess that our hearts are often troubled and our minds are often afraid.
We confess that in our own struggles, we are unaware of others. Of their fears and their struggles.

We confess that we inflict our fear on those we love, we inflict our control, we withhold our mercy.

Forgive us God.
Forgive us our offenses and we'll work on forgiving others.
We offer to you our sense of control.
We offer to you our time while we wait.

We ask you to give us glimpses of your glory as we lift our eyes to you.

May it be so.

+++

Acts 16:9-15; Revelation 21:10, 22-22:5; John 14:23-29

A prayer for the seventh Sunday of Easter

God.
We want someone to say, "Come." To invite us in as if we are
expected and wanted and welcome.

After a long journey, after a hard night's work, after a fight,
after a big complicated celebration, we want to be welcomed.
We are thirsty from the desert of surgery and chemo, the desert
of abandonment and rejection, the desert of struggle and
meaninglessness, and we want a sip of life. We want to be known.

We confess.
We confess that we know you tell us that we are loved,
but we don't believe you.
We confess that we know you offer us hope and health,
but we don't believe you.
Or we look at what you offer, and we say,
"I don't want that kind of health. I want to be fixed my way."
We confess that we pretend we aren't thirsty,
because we think your offer has strings.
We confess that we pretend we don't need you.

But we do.

We need your living water and your presence. We need to know that you know us. We need you.

Forgive us, we ask, our trespasses as we are learning from you to forgive others.

Help us to love others the way that you love us.

Hot and tired and thirsty.

And welcome.

Amen.

+++

Acts 16:16-34; Revelation 22:12-21; John 17:20-26

A prayer for Pentecost Sunday

God.

You are here.
We forget.
We make plans and then we ask you to make them happen.
We call it asking you to bless them.

But you heard them all along.

On some of them, you made suggestions and we listened.
On some of them, you made suggestions and we ignored.
On some of them, you long ago said, "don't do that," but we did anyway and asked you to bless our plans, to make them happen.

We confess to forgetting that you already know our plans.
We confess to forgetting that we seldom think about your plans.
We confess that we expect you to do what we say and get upset when you don't.
We confess that we read the story of Pentecost and forget, Holy Spirit, that you are here, now, in this place, as much as you were

there, then, in that place.

We confess that you are here.

Spirit, we ask the Father in the name of the Son, that you will make us aware of your presence. We ask that you will teach us and remind us of what Jesus said. We ask that we will be full of your power in the same way that we are already full of your presence, that we will be aware of your guidance in the middle of our planning instead of at the end, that we will be honest in our confession and filled with joy in our confession.

May it be so.

+++

Acts 2:1-21; Romans 8:14-17; John 14:8-27

A prayer for Trinity Sunday and the beginning of Ordinary Time

God.

We crave wisdom.
We want to know the next thing to do.
We want to know that the next thing to do is the best thing,
is the right thing,
is the thing that will mean something.

Is the thing that will help us, will help others, will help you.

We want to know why this hurts, why this matters, why this happened to us.

We confess that, actually, we want answers more than we want wisdom.
We confess that, actually,
we want comfort more than we want wisdom,
comfort for now more than wisdom for always.
We confess that we want the easy thing to do more than the hard

best thing to do.

We confess that we crave us as much as we crave wisdom.

Forgive us, God.

Forgive us the ways that we have chosen us rather than others this week.

Forgive us the ways that we have chosen us and others rather than you this week.

Forgive us the ways that we have done what we knew wasn't wise, or didn't do what we knew was wise.

Perhaps, God, we need to crave courage more than wisdom, more than comfort.

Perhaps, God, we need to crave you more than anything.

Perhaps, God, we simply need to stop craving and start accepting you.

God in three persons, God almighty, Lord Jesus Christ, Spirit of truth.

As we begin Ordinary Time, the days and weeks between Pentecost and Advent, help us to hear what you say, do what you say, rest in what you say.

Help us accept your love for us.

May it be so.

+++

Proverbs 8:1–4, 23–31; Romans 5:1–5

A prayer for the twelfth Sunday in Ordinary Time

God.

Elijah lived a long time ago. But he isn't so different.
He wanted to be safe.
He wondered why you let him down.
He was exhausted.
He wondered why bad people had the power.
He was afraid.
He wanted to tell you his complaint more than he wanted to hear your explanation.

We confess that we are like Elijah, sometimes.
We do good things. We expect good results.
We see your power for others. We predict how it should work for us.
We confess that we are unwilling to trust in you.

We confess that we are like the man possessed,
That we can't think right, that we need your release and relief,

we need your healing for our souls and hearts more, perhaps, than your healing for our bodies.

At least as much as for our bodies.

We confess we don't know what you want, other than our faith.

Our faith that you are, that you listen, that you are listening right now.

Hear our cry, Lord God.

Hear our deep longing for you.

And help us receive the healing and hope you offer, not demanding the kind we want.

Because your healing heals us completely.

Your hope carries our hearts.

You, and you alone, God, are God.

Through Christ our Lord,

Amen.

+++

1 Kings 19:1-15; Psalm 42; Luke 8:26-39

A prayer for the thirteenth Sunday in Ordinary Time

God.

We need you.

Even when we don't think we do, we need you.
Not so much to fix things, which is what we think we want: fix my relationships, fix my body, fix my car.
We don't so much need to you to do things, move mountains, make miracles, save me.
We need you to love us and to welcome us and to care about us.

Because, God, we could live with a broken car if we knew for sure that you knew, and that you cared, and that you were powerful.

Are powerful, I mean. I don't want to say that wrong. I don't want you to think that I am saying the wrong words, that I am not recognizing you.

We confess that we worry about saying things wrong.
We confess that we worry about getting things right.

We confess that we haven't figured out what you really meant by "love your neighbor as yourself" after two millennia of trying.
We confess that we don't often enough ask you for help in understanding what it means.

And so, on our behalf, I ask for help.
Help us today to love in the self-surrendering, other-serving, Father-directed way you loved, Jesus.
Help us see clearly those who have served you well and pick up their mantle and work with all the strength you give us to love deeply the ones you created.

And died for.
And live with.

May we keep in step with you.

Amen.

+++

2 Kings 2:1-2, 6-14; Galatians 5:1, 13-25; Luke 9:5-62

A prayer for the fourteenth Sunday in Ordinary Time

God.

We are in a hospital. We want to be healed.
We would almost be willing to dip ourselves in a dirty river if you would guarantee that we would be healed.

We confess.

We confess that we'd rather have one big miracle and be done than have tiny steps of obedience.
We confess that we prefer to reap what someone else has sowed than to spend all that time ourselves.
We confess that we are tempted to judge more than we are committed to love.
We find it harder to forgive than to condemn.
We find it harder to do what you tell us than it is to tell you what to do.
We confess that even when we are doing the right things, we get weary, we get tired of always being helpful, of often being alone.

We confess that we feel like giving up.

We confess that we need to know that you forgive us and love us.

God.

We ask you for courage.

We ask for the courage to love, to obey, to help.

We ask for the courage to forgive, to persist, to rest.

We ask for the courage to trust, to care, to confess.

We ask for the courage to find our identity in being loved by you.

And we thank you that you listen to us, with compassion for our weakness, because you understand.

Through Christ our Lord,

Amen.

+++

2 Kings 5:1-14; Galatians 6:1-16; Luke 10:1-20

A prayer for rest on the fifteenth Sunday in Ordinary Time

God.

We need rest.
Not sleep, not distraction, not medication, not relief.
We need rest.

We hear you say, Jesus, "Come to me all you who are weary and burdened, and I will give you rest."
We long for rest, but we confess we're not sure we can come with our burdens.

We confess.
We confess that we are afraid that you will scold us rather than giving us rest.
We confess that we are likely to scold others for not giving us rest.
We confess that we are afraid that you will remind us that we took on the burdens.
We confess that we stay away from you until we fix things.
We confess that it's not working.

And so together we hold our weariness out to you.

We acknowledge that we are weary and burdened in body and mind and soul and heart.

We acknowledge that our weariness and burdens make it hard to focus on you.

We acknowledge that you know this and understand this and are compassionate and faithful and forgiving and real.

So we again say,
we need rest.

May we rest in you, today and always.

Amen.

+++

Amos 7:7-15; Colossians 4:1-4; Luke 10:25-37

A prayer for the sixteenth Sunday in Ordinary Time

God.

It's been a long week.

We know that it's been exactly the same 168 hours that every week has, but you know that the feeling of time is different than the counting of time.

You know that minutes spent waiting for answers are longer than days spent living with the answers.

Paul talks about the hope of glory, and I think he's talking about a confidence that comes from the certain anticipation of being with you in your glory.

We confess that we don't have much confidence.

And we confess that we are more certain of grief than we are of glory.

We are more certain of pain than we are of your presence.

We are more certain of our inadequacy, for just about anything,

than we are certain of your adequacy, Jesus. Your adequacy to restore a confident relationship with you, God, in your fullness.

We confess that the words from Amos often describe our lives.
We are more anxious to get busy than we are to rest.
We are more anxious to get a deal than to think about the way our deal will affect the lives of others.
I am more anxious for cheap coffee than I am for fair wages for the family that grows the coffee.
I confess that some days I'm more proud that I spoke in church than I am convicted by not doing what you spoke to me.

Forgive us, we ask.
Or maybe, more accurately, help us accept your forgiveness.
Help us accept your peace.
Help us continue in our faith in your words.
Including believing that you really do love us.

We ask these things through Christ our Lord.

Amen.

+++

Amos 8:1–12; Colossians 1:15–28

A prayer for seventeenth Sunday in Ordinary Time, or any time we don't understand

God.

We don't understand.

Those words describe someone's heart at any given moment somewhere in this hospital.

We don't understand why the treatment isn't working. Or why it is working.

We don't understand why they are still together after 68 years. Or why this relationship isn't working.

We don't understand why so many things are happening to us right now.

We don't understand what the next step is, what you are trying to do here, why you took their child, his joy, her pain.

We confess that we don't understand.

It's not a sin to not understand. I say that all the time.

We confess means we acknowledge, we agree with you.

But we confess that we often don't agree with you, and we're upset.

We confess that we don't understand why you told Hosea who to marry.

Because, we confess, we judge her for her choices.

We confess that we've made assumptions about Gomer, about you, about people all around us, assumptions about bad motives and unjust behaviors.

We confess, we acknowledge, that we get upset with you when you don't explain yourself, justify yourself, do what we think would be best.

We confess that when we don't understand, we ignore you and make up our own answers.

We confess that we forget that you have power and forgiveness, understanding and compassion, both the desire and the direction to grow us.

We don't understand why you care about us or where that care will take us or how this particular part of the story will turn out or who you are helping us become.

For today, help us be strengthened by understanding that when we don't understand, you understand that. And love us.

Through Christ our Lord we are with you.

Amen.

+++

Hosea 1:2-10; Colossians 2:6-19

A prayer for the eighteenth Sunday in Ordinary Time

God.

I think that we don't know where you are working. And we don't know how you are working. Because when you don't do what we would like you to do in the way we would like it done, we think that you aren't working at all. That you are ignoring us.

And we even think that you don't care.

You talk to the people of the tribe of Ephraim with such compassion: "It was I who taught you to walk. It was I who healed you."

But we don't see you guiding *us*. Drawing people together, calling people toward you. We don't see that you have given us minds that respond differently to different kinds of needs, hearts that break differently to different oppressions and injustices. Together, we could be so aware of you and filled with you and working alongside you.

But we confess.

We confess that we lie to each other.
We confess that we are easily angered at things that don't matter.
We confess that we desire more than we need, that we worship more than you.
We confess that we set our minds, set our priorities on things that are not of value.
We confess that we think more about the next episode to watch than the people at the next table over, the next selfie than the next soul over.
We confess that we choose to see the divisions more than we see the image of the creator.

Forgive us, God.

And help us to put on the us you see and are constantly renewing to look more and more like you. So that when we look at ourselves and when we look at others almost all we can see is you.

And maybe that will help us stop hitting and hating each other.

Through Christ our Lord we ask,

Amen.

+++

Hosea 11:1-11; Colossians 3:1-11

A prayer for the nineteenth Sunday in Ordinary Time

God.

We know that this life we see is not all there is.

We read that in the Bible.
We hear that from our friends.
We believe it most of the time.
We want to have confidence in what we hope for and assurance about what we do not see.
There is what we see and what we cannot.
There is who we see and *you* we cannot.
There is where we are and where we will be.

But we confess, we forget that the life we see is not all there is.
In our distraction, we forget. Through our own inattention and the intentional distraction by others, we forget to hope for you. Forgive us.

In our good fortune, we forget. We forget that our gifts are not from us, the place we were born was not our choice, our current comfort is not a guarantee, nor is it to be our goal. Forgive us.

In our bad fortune we forget. We blame you, we blame others, we look for scapegoats, we ignore our responsibility for bad choices. We forget that what feels bad in this moment is often good in the next. Forgive us.

In our pain we forget. Because pain is real and sometimes all we can do in the moment of our pain is cry out. Forgive us for blaming ourselves for not being more spiritual, forgive us for thinking we are better than you, Jesus, who cried out in your pain.

In our loss we forget. Because death is real separation, because sudden death is so sudden, the thought of life extending after death often doesn't comfort us at the moment. Forgive us for inflicting judgment on ourselves and others in times of loss.

And comfort us Spirit, with the truth that is present when we don't feel it.

Help our faith, just as you helped Abel and Noah and Abraham in the moments when they wavered. Because they were people like us. And you are God like then.

Through Christ our Lord,

Amen.

+++

Isaiah 1:1, 10-20; Hebrews 11:1–16

A prayer for the twentieth Sunday in Ordinary Time

God.

We're stopped now.

Our bodies at rest, sitting or standing, or lying here. But our minds are not at rest, racing around a track to catch understanding of what is happening, why we are in this situation, now, in this place. Our hearts are beating faster with the adrenaline of fear of what could have happened, what might happen, what has happened.

We are stopping, but we are not at rest.

We are afraid that for all our work, we do not have good grapes, and so we worry harder. We are afraid that our difficulties are punishment for bad work, for not paying attention, and so we promise to do more. We are fearful and frustrated that our small steps are not big enough to change the problems we are facing fast enough. We are afraid that pain and death will be more than we

can endure.
We are afraid.

We confess.
We confess that we haven't talked to you about this sooner.
We confess that we haven't seen that our work is a response to your graciousness, not a cause for it.
We confess that we haven't listened for your love as much as we have feared your lecture.
We confess that we aren't sure exactly what to confess, but we're sure there must be something awful. Otherwise, you would do more to make us happy. Which is another thing to confess. The belief that we should be happier.
We confess that knowing about all the people who lived and died living in faith doesn't give us courage as much as make us feel bad for how little faith we must have.

Forgive us, God.
Or better, help us accept the forgiveness we already have through Jesus.
Help us accept the love with which you see us, the identity we have in you, the courage you offer.
Help us fix our eyes on you, Jesus, who walked through death and resurrection first and best.
Help us see you all the way through.

Amen.

+++

Isaiah 5:1–7; Hebrews 11:29–12:2

A prayer for the twenty-first Sunday in Ordinary Time

God.

We hear Jeremiah's words to you and they could be our words.

You spoke to him. You said, "I know you." You said, "Speak for me."
Jeremiah said, "I don't know how to speak. I am too young."

You speak to us and we say, "I'm too young. I'm too old. I'm too uncertain. I'm too different. I'm too tired. I'm too outside the cool people. I'm too ignorant. I'm too confused. I'm too involved with these other things you gave me to do."

But what we are really saying is what Jeremiah was really saying: "I'm too afraid."

We're afraid of others. We are afraid of ourselves. We are afraid of you. We are afraid we will say the wrong things to the wrong people in the wrong way. We are afraid we will be condemned or shamed or ignored. We are afraid we will say something is from you, and it will be from us. We are afraid we will tell people you will do something, and then you won't. Like healing our loved one. Like rescuing our hearts. Like saving our lives.

We confess that we are afraid of you.
We confess that we see you more like Moses saw you on Mount Sinai than like the writer of Hebrews saw you on Mount Zion.
Welcoming with open arms and hole-marked hands.
Powerful for us not against us.
Surrounded by delighted angels inviting us to join the delight.
Joined in reality, though not yet visibly, to a whole community of people from the criminal on the cross to my dad, from Mary and Mary and Mary to my grandma Hazel.
We confess that we forget you love us and them. And we confess that we forget that you have and are and will forgive us our trespasses as we forgive those who have trespassed against us.

Remind us of your powerful presence. Help us respond with thankfulness rather than defensiveness, holiness rather than hollowness, hospitality for others rather than arrogance for getting it right.

Because the life you give us, the healing you give us, the message you give us is for the good of others, not just us.

We ask this through Christ our Lord.

Amen.

+++

Jeremiah 1:4-10; Hebrews 12:18-29

A prayer for the twenty-second Sunday in Ordinary Time

God.

We think we talk to you all the time. We ask you for protection for family in the path of the hurricane. We ask you to keep our loved one from dying in the emergency room. We ask you for jobs and health and money and relief. Then we talk about you not showing up. Or we talk about you not listening. Or we talk about our prayer not working.

God, I'm not sure that we show up to you. I'm not sure we are listening for you. I'm not sure that our prayer works. Because I'm not sure that we are talking to you as much as we are talking to ourselves.

You said to Jeremiah that your people made two mistakes, that they committed two sins. They ignored you, the spring of living water, and they made their own leaky cisterns.

I confess. For us all.
We do forget that you are the source of living water and think

you are the source of our comfort.

We want you to heal what we want healed when you want to heal what is actually wounded.

We want you to fix what we want fixed when you want to mend what is actually broken.

We want you to bless what we want blessed when you want to forgive what we need to repent of.

God, help us let down our guard. God, help us let down our pride. God, help us let down our fear.

God, help us.

We offer to you what isn't working about the ways we are running our lives. We accept from you forgiveness. We accept from you the offer to do your work with your power in your presence, which is everywhere. Because you never leave us, you never forsake us, you never disappear.

But you aren't our idol. You are our God. You aren't made in our image, we are made in yours. You aren't our coffee mug, contained for our convenience.

But we do ask for your protection and your peace. Because you don't scold us for talking with you.

Through Christ our Lord,
Amen.

+++

Jeremiah 2:4–13; Hebrews 13:1–8, 15–16

A prayer for the twenty-third Sunday in Ordinary Time

God.

You know us. You know all about us.
You make us inside and out.
You are completely aware of the things we are good at and the things we struggle with.
You are aware of the things that annoy us about ourselves.
You are aware of our insecurities and our anxieties, our adequacies and our competencies.
You are aware of what you have equipped us to be able to do, yet you don't disown us when we don't measure up.

In fact, you don't actually measure. Not like we do.

You know us and are willing to watch us grow, to help us grow.
You are willing to give our willingness shape, to take our efforts and weave them into the cloth than can comfort crying babies and broken hearts.
You know us and are willing to guide us when we need wisdom,

to comfort us when we know pain, to restore us when we come back from wandering.

You love us more than we can imagine.

But we confess.

We confess that we don't believe that you love us that much.
We confess that we feel more like Onesimus the rebellious slave than like Onesimus the forgiven servant.
We confess that we are more interested in fixing ourselves poorly than in letting you transform us.

Forgive us.

Help us.

Keep talking, please, as you will.

Through the amazing work of Christ our Lord,

Amen.

+++

Jeremiah 18:1-11; Philemon 1-21

A prayer for the twenty-fourth Sunday in Ordinary Time

God.

It's hard for us to understand that you are God, and we are not.
It's hard to remember that we don't have to do everything.
It's hard for some of us to stop and laugh and rest and not be productive. Forgetting that being productive means stopping and laughing and resting.
And, on this morning, letting someone else preach.
And on this morning, running a 5K in Grand Rapids.

Thank you for Dan, who is preaching.
Thank you for Nancy.
Thank you for Andrew and Allie and Hope and Dan.
Thank you for health for the moment and strength for the moment.
Thank you for things I can't describe here.
Thank you for the people who are reading these words.

God, on this day, and always, forgive them, bless them, and speak to them in the way that they know that it's you.

Through Christ our Lord,

Amen.

A prayer for the twenty-fifth Sunday in Ordinary Time

God.

Sometimes we feel like we ache all the time because of the pain we see around us.
Sometimes we feel like we are crushed.
Sometimes we feel like weeping like Jeremiah wept.

And we struggle to know how to talk to you when even the experts seem to disagree.

Because Paul tells Timothy to pray for those in authority, and Jeremiah weeps because of the destruction that came from those in authority.
Paul tells Timothy that God wants all people to be saved and Jeremiah weeps because of the crushing of the people of God.
And, as we read those words, we think about our loved ones and those we don't know but hear of.
Those who are ill, those who are dying,

those who are oppressed, those who are oppressing,
those who are wandering, and those who are wondering.

We are at a loss.

We confess that we feel powerless to do anything.
We confess that we feel more overwhelmed by pressure than we
feel aware of your power.
We confess that we feel more adrift than we feel embraced by you.

God.

Please let us know that you are with us.
Please let us know your healing power.
Please help us remember that Jesus is with us and with you,
And please give all your people peace from all those in authority
all over the world.

Through Christ our Lord,

Amen.

+++

Jeremiah 8:19-9:1; 1 Timothy 2:1-7

A prayer on the twenty-sixth Sunday in Ordinary Time

God.

If I were home today, I'd be praying a little and preaching a little. I'd have to study, have to write, have to pray.

But Dan is handling all those things for me today, reading your words, praying your words, reflecting out loud on your words.

"Some people, eager for money, have wandered from the faith and pierced themselves with many griefs. But you, [Timothy], flee from all this, and pursue righteousness, godliness, faith, love, endurance and gentleness."

It's part of a letter, God, that you encouraged Paul to write to Timothy, to remind him of what you and Paul knew would matter most to his work.

I wonder, God, whether Timothy felt the itch to work hard because he knew lack from growing up in a single parent home. I wonder whether he worried about not working, whether he struggled with vacation because it meant that he wasn't making anything, that he was depending on the good will of other people. I wonder whether that urge for responsibility ever edged into being eager for money.

But God, it doesn't matter why you and Paul cautioned him.
What matters is what you set in front of him to run toward, to be devoted to: *Righteousness. Godliness. Faith. Love. Endurance. Gentleness.*

Boundaries to guide his decisions.
Quests to guide his imagination.
Missions to structure his whole life.
Character elements to build the way Andrew built endurance for his race, the way Hope builds depth of flavor and color in cakes. With diligence and devotion and occasional delight.

God, this week, could you help me, help my friends, see small forward steps in gentleness in particular, but your righteousness, faith, and love as well.

Help us to be like you, help us to last all week long.

Amen.

+++

Jeremiah 32:1–15; 1 Timothy 6:6–19

A prayer for the twenty-seventh Sunday in Ordinary Time

God.

We need you.

We need something or someone to anchor us.
We need something or someone to steady us.
We need something or someone to stop changing all the time.

Because everyone and everything is changing all the time.

We are fretting. On account of evil doers.
And we aren't sure who the evil doers are anymore.
Because the people we thought we should trust, those in charge,
those who you gave charge to, are fully human.
Are they scheming or are they planning?
Are they serving us or you or themselves?
Are they in love with you or with the idea of love?
Are they we?

We confess that we are timid.

We confess that we respond more to public opinions than to your clear simple invitations.

We confess that we worry more about how things will turn out than we remember your clear simple declarations: "our Saviour, Christ Jesus, who has destroyed death and has brought life and immortality to light through the gospel."

We confess that we don't always understand that clarity, and we don't always believe that death has been destroyed, and we don't always see life and light.

And we confess that we really don't understand the Gospel,

Not in its richness and abundance and power.

But, we confess, we really want to.

May we know your forgiveness.

May we know your salvation.

May we know your calling.

May we know your power and love and self-control.

May we know you.

Even in the rubble.

Even in the pain.

Even in the present.

Through Christ our Lord, we ask,

Amen.

+++

Psalm 37; Lamentations 1:1-6; 2 Timothy 1:1-14

A prayer for the twenty-eighth Sunday in Ordinary Time

God.

We feel forgotten.

We know that we should remember that you are with us. We know that we should turn to you and be comforted by you when we are in trouble. We know that we feel abandoned by you. We are sure that it's our fault, the abandonment, or your fault, the abandonment. And we don't know what to do.

We confess.
We confess that we've been frustrated by where we have ended up.
We confess that we've looking around for someone to blame.
We confess that we've remembered some of your words, but have assumed that they weren't true.
We confess that we feel abandoned by you, our prayers ignored by you, our good work discounted by you.
We confess that we feel a little exiled.

And we confess that we cannot understand how Paul can be so confident about you when he's chained to a smelly, obnoxious Roman guard.

We confess that we are often derailed by bad coffee, by long lines, by annoying things we read.

Thank you that you forgive us.

Thank you that you invited us to work for the good of the people who are working for our bad.

Thank you that you are faithful toward us even when we don't have any faith ourselves.

Thank you that your mercy doesn't depend on our merit, that your grace doesn't depend on our goodness, that your calling doesn't depend on our competence.

Thank you that you are always more than enough of a God for us.

Help us remember that when we are failing at being our own gods.

Help us be helpful when we are away from our comfort.

Help us have fun, as you told the people in exile.

Through Christ our Lord,

Amen.

+++

Jeremiah 29:4–7; 2 Timothy 2:8–15

A prayer for the twenty-ninth Sunday in Ordinary Time

God.

We are weary and worried and wishful.
We are weary from all the voices and all the choices and all the things that break.
We are worried from all the stories of what might go wrong and who might go wrong.
We are wishful for escape and order and answers.

We're not sure whether it helps to know that your people have been weary and worried and wishful for thousands of years.

When we know that this is human, it is a little helpful.
When we know that you haven't fixed it yet, it's not helpful.
And we want something that is helpful in our weariness, hopeful in our worry.

We confess.
We confess that we are more like Timothy's audience than we are like Timothy, gathering voices that scratch what our ears are

itching to hear.

We confess that we look for people who agree with us more than we look for people who challenge us.

We confess that we want to blame other's choices for the sour taste in our mouths, forgetting that we ate the bad grapes, acted on the bad advice, followed the destructive but comfortable path.

We confess that we turn away from giving or receiving careful instruction with great patience.

Forgive us, God, as you have been forgiving your people for thousands of years.

Remind us of your gracious calling, your forgiving presence, your life-giving words, expressed in Jesus, the living Word, and carried to us in your written word.

Open our minds and our hearts to your loving law.

Through Christ our Lord we ask,

Amen.

+++

Jeremiah 31:27–34; 2 Timothy 3:14–4:5

A prayer for the thirtieth Sunday in Ordinary Time

God.

We are not quite ready to despair, most of us.

But some moments we come close.
We come close to simply running out.
Our bodies run out. Our courage runs out. Our creativity runs out. Our love, our patience, our forgiveness. We are running out. And there is almost nothing we read or watch that gives us deep delight. It mostly distracts and disturbs us.

We confess.
We confess that fatigue feels like failure.
We confess that our anxiety is bigger than our faith.

We acknowledge that our attention shrinks to the size of the pain in front of us, the discomfort we want to remove, the annoyance we are experiencing through no fault of anyone else. And we know that sometimes this is what being human means, that pain overwhelms us.

93

But we confess that sometimes we allow the desire for comfort and the annoyance with others to overwhelm us.

We confess that we want our deepest desire to be for you and that we don't know how to want anything that much.

God, help us.

In our despair, give us your hope.
In our worry, give us your peace.
In our distraction, give us your purpose.
In our fatigue, give us your rest.

In our new day, give us your eternal presence.

Through Christ our Lord,

Amen.

+++

Joel 2:23-32; 2 Timothy 4:6-8, 16-18

A prayer for the thirty-first Sunday in Ordinary Time

God.

We feel disconnected. Isolated. Lonely.

Even when we are with people all day long, helping, serving, working, we feel disconnected.
Even with invisible community connections of chat, we feel lonely.
And when we are away from home, away from routine, away from what we know best and do best, we feel isolated.

We feel far from you.
We feel like Daniel, a thousand miles from home, in the middle of the night, in the middle of a dream, watching things too great for us, things immense and terrifying. We feel anxious.

We confess.
We confess that we see things we don't understand, and we live in fear of what they mean.
We confess that we are more lonely that we want to admit, but

we are less willing to build bridges to others than we could be.

We confess that we hear that you are immeasurably great but we don't know how to believe it.

We don't know how to allow that knowledge to change our hearts and change our minds and change the direction of our hands.

To hope rather than always hesitating.

To try rather than always trembling.

To rest rather than always wrestling.

To come into community rather than fearing condemnation.

Because we really want to be in community with others, with you in common.

With purpose rather than pettiness.

With forgiveness rather than failure.

With fun rather than franticness.

With rest rather that restlessness.

God, we want to know that we are part of your body, from all time for all time. And to find our identity, to find who we are, in you.

Through Christ our Lord,

Amen.

+++

Daniel 7:1-3; 15-18; Ephesians 1:11-23

A prayer for the thirty-second Sunday
in Ordinary Time

God.

It's so easy to lose track. Of our plans, of our direction, of you.

One fall, one fracture, one hospital stay, one cold, two bad nights of sleep and the lists we had and the projects we were working toward get lost.

It's hard to keep our quiet routines as our time is tied to hospital time.
"Soon" is ninety minutes.
"Not sure until I look" puts the day into uncertainty.
The visits that come with random regularity make it almost impossible to maintain a train of thought.

And as much as I trust you, I'm aware that someone always has to be the 1% or the side effects or the not quite right.

I forget completely Paul's blessing to the Thessalonians:

"Now may our Lord Jesus Christ Himself and God our Father,
who has loved us and given us eternal comfort and good hope by grace,
comfort and strengthen your hearts in every good work and word."

Help us to remember that we don't forget you when our times are out of our hands.
Offer us your comfort and strengthen our hearts as we live through what life is, festivals and falls, coffee and colds, hospitality and healthcare and unexpected interruptions and unforeseen affirmations.

Through Christ our Lord,

Amen.

+++

Haggai 1:15-2:9; 2 Thessalonians 2:1-5, 13-17

A prayer for the thirty-third Sunday in Ordinary Time

God.

We are a sad and fearful people.

Not all of us, of course. Some of us some of the time are happy and confident. And we don't want to be fearful.
But all of us know that we will face pain and will face death.
And it shapes our thinking.
Sometimes we work hard to avoid pain.
Sometimes we work hard to ignore life.
We mostly wish we were better at accepting life.

We confess.
We confess that we have spent more time this week worrying about what might happen than we have celebrating what we could celebrate.
We confess that we have had moments where we identify with the unruly, undisciplined, busybodies of Thessalonika.
We confess that we grow weary of doing good. Probably because

it looks more fun to be unruly, undisciplined busybodies.

We confess that we are fearful, and we'd rather not talk to you about our real deep fears because we'd have to acknowledge them out loud.

We confess that we are afraid you won't find us good enough, because no one else does.

We confess that we are afraid that we would have to change for you to love us, to notice us.

And we confess that we are afraid that if we don't change enough, you will cut us off.

But, you paint a picture for Isaiah of a place that knows about pain and weakness and weeping and responds with healing.

You paint a picture where everything works, and it is for your people. It is for us.

God, we want to hope in that kind of place.

Help us accept your love for us.
Help us look more at you than the news.
Help us see you in our moment of need. And always.

Through Christ our Lord,

Amen.

+++

Isaiah 65: 17–25; 2 Thessalonians 3:6–13

A prayer for Christ the King Sunday

God.

We are skeptical of kings.
We are skeptical of political answers to our problems.

But the truth is, we are skeptical about any answers to our problems. Some of us are skeptical about most things.
We work, and other people win.
We pray, and people we love are still sick.
We love, and we are misunderstood.
We try, and we are tired from trying.

We think, perhaps, we are not wholehearted enough. We've heard enough church leaders and political leaders and coaches tell us that our problem is that we are half-hearted.

We keep trying.

But really, we aren't so much half-hearted as broken-hearted.
We've trusted leaders and been betrayed.
We've trusted shepherds and been misled.
We've trusted ourselves and come undone.

Christ, we read that in you all things hold together.
We know that means some big creation thing. But what we want, deep down, is that in you our hearts might hold together.

Christ, we read in you all powers were created.
We know that means some fullness of time thing. But what we want, deep down, is that our minds might find rest in understanding that your big intention is true even in our current frustrations and pain.

Christ, we read that you are reconciling all things to yourself.
We know that means some big theological truth. But what we want, deep down, is to know that you want us, that you are drawing us close to you. Close to your heart. Close to your side. Close to your throne.

Help us today to understand that all our pictures of you as king are like childish sketches, reacting to the failures around us more than your trueness.

Help us know that you are King above kings, Lord above parties, Creator above creatives, Shepherd above shepherds, God above us.

Heal our hearts. Rule in our lives. Help us.

Through Christ our Lord,

Amen.

+++

Jeremiah 23:1-6; Colossians 1:11-20

Afterword by Fr. James Bromwich

The knock on the window woke me up. As the priest, I got the bunk near the window so I could get up to visit someone without waking the others. It felt like I had been sleeping five minutes. It was more like an hour.

After the 2010 earthquake in Haiti, which killed about 250,000 people and inflicted incalculable injuries, both physical and emotional on others, our little Catholic hospital north of Port au Prince served the injured and their families. I was with a team of first responders.

This night, a 17-year old girl was declining rapidly. Her brother, along with a couple of other relatives, were anxiously waiting news in the courtyard waiting area. Her brother was being hit particularly hard. I briefly greeted them when I arrived but could not stop long. First things first. There were only two medical personnel in the room: a physician and a nurse. I was needed in my role as nurse first. She needed to be coded. We were severely limited in what we could do since we did not have a ventilator. Our first round was successful. She was stabilized and we quietly celebrated. Within minutes, however, this young lady began a

103

rapid decline. Our hearts sank. We could do nothing more for her but pray and watch her die. Two of us began praying the Divine Mercy Chaplet, a traditional prayer at the hour of death. She died within minutes.

We found the family in the hospital's courtyard and broke the news. It was devastating, especially for the brother of the deceased. Ultimately, he needed psychiatric assistance, including medication to calm him. All I could do was sit quietly with him and be present. I kept saying, "I am sorry. I'm so sorry." These were the few words I knew in his language. I must have sat there next to him for close to an hour. Before I left, the brother looked me intently in the eyes and asked me to pray. I prayed the only prayer I knew in French, the Our Father (in Haiti, Catholics speak Haitian Creole, but pray in French). It seemed I had done little for the family, but I had done all that was needed: to be present and to care.

Two hours later (or was it one, or three?) I walked the short distance back to our residence. I was overwhelmed with emotion. As I stopped and looked up into the sky I suddenly realized, through my tears, that my faith was stronger than it had ever been. "How could my faith actually increase amidst all this suffering?" I asked myself rhetorically. Walking with others in their suffering is to walk with Jesus and let him walk with me. I experienced what I had been teaching for years. I thanked God for that moment.

Loving God, you who are our sure foundation, we come to you with so many needs. We are powerless in many ways. So often we do not know what to do for others in their trials. To be present with others in times of need is to be your presence. Help us never forget that the smallest gesture offered in love can bring hope to someone's life. Help us to remember that often all you ask of us is to show up and be present. Most of all, Loving Father, increase our faith, especially amidst suffering. We ask this through Christ, our Lord. Amen.

+++

Fr. James Bromwich is a Catholic priest, mission leader in healthcare, storyteller and a good friend.

About the Author

Rev. Jon Swanson has been talking with God for nearly six decades. Although he has a PhD in rhetorical theory, he's pretty sure that persuading God is neither possible nor preferable. He's an ordained pastor with 15 years in church ministry. He's spent more than 20 years in higher education, teaching communication, management, and spiritual formation, and working as an administrator. Most recently, he's worked as a hospital chaplain in a Level II Trauma Center, and adjunct professor, and a consultant with churches and non-profits.

Nancy and Jon have been married since 1983 and have two married children and a daughter in heaven. They've walked regularly since 2006, and he started running in 2014.

If this book has been helpful, please leave a review on Amazon: *"God. We Need You": A Year of Prayer in a Hospital Chapel.*

Also by Jon Swanson

Books (all available at anewroutine.com)

Anticipation: An Advent Reader (2012)

Learning A New Routine. Reading the Sermon on the Mount a Little Bit at a Time (2012)

Lent for Non-Lent People: 33 Things to Give up for Lent and Other Readings (2013)

A Great Work: A Conversation With Nehemiah For People (Who Want To Be) Doing Great Works (2013)

Saint John of the Mall: Reflections for the Advent Season (2017)

Giving a Life Meaning: How to Lead Funerals, Memorial Services, and Celebrations of Life. (2020)

Before You Walk In: A Devotional Primer for Chaplains and Pastoral Visitors (2020) at beforeyouwalkin.com.

Blogs

300wordsaday.com – I write six days a week about following God. Each Sunday is a prayer, just like the prayers in this book.

socialmediachaplain.com – I write regularly about caring for others, particularly in hospitals.

Resources on Faith, Sickness, Grief, and Doubt

In 2017, Patrick Riecke started working on his second book, about talking with sick, dying, and grieving people.[1] It was clear to him that this wasn't going to be one book about faith and doubt, sickness and grief. His experience as a pastor and chaplain and leader and grieving father told him that this needed to be the first in a series of resources.

With the book you are holding, there are now five books in the series. Each book is practical and honest, with explanations and resources based in personal and professional experience. To find the latest books in this series and other helpful resources, visit EmeraldHopePublishing.com

Patrick Riecke, *How to Talk With Sick, Dying, and Grieving People: When There Are No Magic Words to Say.* (Fort Wayne, Emerald Hope Publishing House, 2018).

---

1. His first book was his master's degree thesis. He published it as an experiment in publishing.

Patrick Riecke, *How to Find Meaning in Your Life Before it Ends.* (Fort Wayne, Emerald Hope Publishing House, 2019).

Jon Swanson, *Giving a Life Meaning: How to Lead Funerals, Memorial Services, and Celebrations of Life.* (Fort Wayne, Emerald Hope Publishing House, 2020).

Kristen and Patrick Riecke. *No Matter How Small: Understanding Miscarriage and Stillbirth.* (Fort Wayne, Emerald Hope Publishing House, 2020).

Jon Swanson, *"God. We Need You": A Year of Prayer in a Hospital Chapel.* (Fort Wayne, Emerald Hope Publishing House, 2020).

Made in the USA
Monee, IL
02 October 2020